THE
LIGHTNING
THAT STRIKES
THE
NEIGHBORS'
HOUSE

THE FELIX POLLAK PRIZE IN POETRY

THE
LIGHTNING
THAT STRIKES
THE
NEIGHBORS'
HOUSE

NICK LANTZ

THE UNIVERSITY OF WISCONSIN PRESS

The University of Wisconsin Press
1930 Monroe Street, 3rd Floor
Madison, Wisconsin 53711-2059
uwpress.wisc.edu

3 Henrietta Street
London WC2E 8LU, England
www.eurospanbookstore.com

5   4   3   2   1

Printed in the United States of America

Library of Congress Cataloging-in-Publication Data
Lantz, Nick.
  The lightning that strikes the neighbors' house / Nick Lantz.
      p. cm. — (Felix Pollak prize in poetry)
  Poems.
  ISBN 978-0-299-23584-0 (pbk.: alk. paper) — ISBN 978-0-299-23583-3 (e-book)
  I. Title. II. Series: Felix Pollak prize in poetry (Series)
  PS3612.A586L54   2010
  811'.6—dc22
                        2009040095

FOR VICKY

CONTENTS

ACKNOWLEDGMENTS

First, I would like to thank the Wisconsin Institute for Creative Writing for its generous support during my time as a Jay C. and Ruth Halls Poetry Fellow, 2007–8.

Some of these poems first saw the light of day in MFA workshops, and for their help I would like to thank my fellow MFAs: Lisa Marie Brodsky, David Camphouse, Kevin González, Emily Green, and Rita Mae Reese. I also owe a debt of deep gratitude to the wonderful University of Wisconsin creative writing faculty.

Thanks are due to the journals that published the following poems:

Locuspoint (online)	"The Marian Apparitions," "SETI," "Love Letter from inside the Titan Missile Museum," "Kuzka's Mother," and "History of Fire"
MARGIE	"The Aging Sci-Fi Actor Speaks to Third Graders at the Local Planetarium"
Mid-American Review	"The Last Words of Pancho Villa"
Prairie Schooner	"The Miracle"
Southern Review	"The Cryptozoologist Chaperones His Daughter's Prom"

Finally, I would especially like to thank Carrie Conners, Cynthia Hoffman, and Jesse Lee Kercheval, through whose careful consideration many of these poems passed; Vicky Lantz, for her support; and my parents, Dona Lantz and Jim Wright, for a lifetime of encouragement.

WHERE YOU ARE,
WHERE YOU'VE BEEN,
WHERE YOU'RE GOING

SHIP OF THESEUS

I wish I could forgive the uglier potatoes on my plate,
      like the wedding dancer so drunk
                      he doesn't notice
when he loses one partner and grabs hold of another.

      The reed warbler goes on feeding
                the cuckoo long after
its own chicks have starved to death. Some days I almost believe
      I could live the life
               of a bowl of plastic fruit.

Why should I visit London Bridge, rebuilt stone by stone
      in Arizona? The childhood ceiling
                I stickered with plastic
stars was no consolation for starless city nights.

      After the fight when you broke
                your finger pounding
on the table, we came back to each other like generals
      in their civvies shaking
                hands years after armistice.

The Athenians cared for their hero's ship, replacing
      each plank as it rotted away,
                until none of the old ship
remained, until no living person had seen the original.

      The helicopter's spotlight, groping
                the dark hillside,
pins a coyote in the blown-back grass, and the animal
      looks up into the light as if to say,
                No, it's not me.

THE WEREWOLF DREAMS
OF LOVE

A hasp, a clasp, a lock heavy as a fossilized
                    lung. The hunters
          line up at the edge of the forest, still

as terracotta soldiers in the prince's tomb.
                    I am the moon's
          litigant, howling like a chainsaw. The smith

in his workshop hammers out rings, keys,
                    weathervanes,
          a mechanical bird. The hunters are wearing

skins; the hunters have no skins. I love
                    you all day,
          and you become a bird with silver bullets

for feathers. I am the field where thieves
                    bury gold
          they will not live to recover. The deer

are breaking branches; the bears sleep
                    like clouds.
          A hunter chasing a deer through the snow

trips on a buried stone wall and shoots
                    off his hand.
          The tribes of grief have propped their buckskin

tents against the wind. The smith ties a chain
                    around the forest;
          inside a golden box he locks the sun. I am

the field where the hunter dies waiting
                    for help. Wild
          dogs are chasing the shadow of a bird back

and forth across a field; their tracks mark
                    a code
          in the snow. I can read only your track,

the parabola cut by your half-lame foot.
                    The smith
          is swallowing all of his rings. I will read

your code: Whose greed? Whose grief?
                    Whose life
          like a window left lit till dawn? Who

standing by the edge of the woods
                    with a handful
          of gold and a leather bag full of teeth?

At night you are a lock on an old barn door,
                    and a farmer
          is grinding an ax inside your skull.

THE DIVING HORSES

You know how the old stories go: the peasant's hut
        grows a little smaller every
                day, the frog by the window
a little louder. It's a miracle we can sleep at all.

        In the hotel room the night after
                    your brother's funeral,
we watched a bad movie about horses trained to jump
        from a platform into a small pool
                        forty feet below.

In the first garden, the fruit didn't know when to drop.
        So what if starvation is the only thing
                    that can make
the young albatross use its wings for the first time?

        Why can't I be more
                like the hermit crab, strutting
around the sea floor in an empty perfume bottle?

        The news cuts in. The president
                    shrugs. So what
if your brother dies? Without the fox's teeth deep
        in the hen's downy neck,
                  we would starve.

After the war, when Sherman took his evening walks,
        the fence posts lay down
                in the grass and trembled.
The horses, we're told, required very little prodding.

LOVE LETTER FROM INSIDE
THE TITAN MISSILE MUSEUM

Down in the silo,
        the hallways rest on springs, everything cushioned by curls of steel. No
bombs or earthquakes can shake us loose. We breathe together, the three-foot-thick
steel door sealed against radiation and poison and daylight. Here, mannequins
enact the many duties of the missing crew. Always two. A rule, they say: no-alone.
Two sit at the launch control, wooden fingertips tense against the knobs and dials
that could have ended us all—no matter how diligently we paired ourselves off. Two
aboveground, in the helicopter, its rotor welded, its skids chained to the cement.
Two repairing a coolant hose in the wall of the silo—the wire holding one up has
snapped, and he has fallen
        into his comrade, as if to embrace him. Down here, suspicion or love
keeps us close. We are spies, we are untrustworthy, we keep secrets close as skin.
How many times have we watched this film, the actors in blue jumpsuits playing
the already absent crew? And how many times will we see the same clip of the
missile launching, the glowing dots that light up across the cold continent of our
birth? Ascending the stairs, we burst blinking into the raw breath of desert sun. We
know little more than when we first peered down the well of the silo—it was so
brightly lit, we saw everything, every tube, panel, girder, and button. But we could
not see the bottom. There was no bottom to see,

                                                though the two of us
                                                looked and looked.

THE MIRACLE

Around the small stone footprint, we built a temple.
        Each new autumn the seedpods
                        split open as before.
No one living today remembers the miracle.

        In the story, God doles out
                duties to each new creature,
but when humans arrive he has nothing left to give.
        Not every stutter
              in the genome is a miracle.

Outside the temple, the statue of a horse weeps all day.
        In each loaf we found a mouse
              baked hard as a peach stone.
Onto their alms bowls, the saints carved the word *miracle*.

        Every spring we took the strongest
                  man in the village
and nailed him to a tree. We paid three women to grieve.
        What other animal hungers
             for such miracles?

The saints once carried around homilies heavy as bricks:
        always beat the beaten dog
              that comes back to you.
Each house we built during those years was a miracle.

        When struck, the statue's limbs
                   yield different notes.
The blind man carves thirty soapstone birds every day,
        each bird more misshapen,
                each one named Miracle.

WHAT THE LATHE WANTS

Those nights you woke to the lathe humming
from your father's basement, aria of wood
        shrilled away, your father cursing
as gouge or chisel

bit too deep: none of it
can be undone.

        Always at dawn,
your father, his beard and hair
still powdered with sawdust, woke you

for another highway that cut
through almond groves or twisted

a switchback up past the timberline.
Always, he stopped the truck

        to poke around a ghost town
or abandoned mine, pacing the dirt,

turning up old nails and shell casings
with his toe. When he stood for an hour

        at a gas station, listening
to the dull exhale of a forest burning beyond
the nearest ridge, you could tell he wanted

        to go over, to see
what the fire was doing.

Once, in the desert, he tipped over a rock
and uncovered a scorpion, its back heaped
        with translucent young.

When he found a hawk
        dead on the highway shoulder, he searched
all that day for the aerie it would never

return to. Beside a snowmelt river
he stooped by a crater of trampled
grass where some
creature had curled
to spend
the night.

And once, a lone sow bear
                broke from the trees
and ambled across the road in front of you,

not stopping to wonder
                about the squealing

brakes or that strange channel cut
through the forest, and your father

turned the truck down a gravel trail
                to follow it. When he
parked and walked off into the woods,

what could you do except follow him?
You found the den
empty, a smell both

dark and sweet
coming from it. How close

your father kneeled beside it, one hand
braced on the rim. If not

                for your fear,
stammering at the last thin edge of sunlight,

he would have gone in,
headfirst.

Only during the dark drive
home did your father begin
speaking of the lathe, the bowl or finial
        he'd ruined in his eagerness
        and cast aside.

If there was some lesson in it, he forgot
to say: he could only speak

        of the blur
of wood and sharpened
blade and a mind bent

at paring away anything
that resisted.

U.S. ROUTE 50, NEVADA, THE LONELIEST ROAD IN AMERICA

It's totally empty. There are no points of interest. We don't recommend it.
—American Automobile Association

We stop at what's left of a novelty ghost town, facade
        of a saloon with no building
                        behind it, double doors
that swing open onto more desert, sage brush, highway.

        Why can't I wear my shortcomings
                   like a dignitary's
purple sash, my misanthropy inscribed in golden
        letters? Why can't I silently
                back out of every room?

I could be the lizard that drops his tail and bolts
        at the first sign of danger. I could
                be the gummy dust
of a lotto scratch card swept into a pile on the diner table.

        At the roadside casino, slot jockeys
                   sit three stools
apart so as not to sap one another's luck. The desert
        offers up one withered tree
             for the lightning to strike.

I could be the last train, skulking past the platform,
        refusing to stop, even as you
                call out to me, even
as you wave and wave your red bandana.

        Born in isolation, a Mormon cricket
                 is a drab brown,
but a swarm hatches in the colors of a sunset. We
        drive over them for miles
             as they flock across the road.

MOTHER'S INTELLIGENT DESIGN

She replaces all the dead pets: the fish
with mammalian names (Floppy, Hector,
Spot), the gunk-eyed kittens, the rodents,
the incautious dog, the heart-attack canary,
lizards limp as mud. Their deaths are tragic,
grisly, frequent: cooked in the heating ducts,
face down in the hot tub, panting blood
under the porch. None live long, but always
some animal is pacing its cage or corner
of the house, and soon you see them not
as separate, but a continuum, a single life
that warps over time: legs to wings, lungs
to gills—terrible as a tree-limb shadow
contorting on your bedroom wall.

PATTERSON-GIMLIN FILM: FRAME 352

A hoax depends. On sunlight, periphery, the angle
          at which hope strikes
                              the eye's surface. Without
the veil, how could Laban have ever married Leah

          to Jacob? The ants that look
                              like wasps are devouring
the moth that looks like an owl's face. Jacob planted
          rods of poplar, hazel, chestnut
                              in sight of the grazing flocks,

and the ewes birthed dark lambs all season.
          When you were seven, your older
                              brother buried cow bones
in the backyard and egged you into digging them up

          with a spoon. Dinosaurs,
                    he said, and you believed him.
This was before methamphetamines, his tooth you found
          on the bathroom tile. God
                              an opalescent light tracing

an impossible course. Along the horizon. A haggard
          creature loping down
                              the aisle of a clearing. You slip
the paper into its chemical broth, and your brother's face

          emerges from nothing, a pale
                              cataract forming
over his shoulder—a ghost, or light leaked in.
          In high school you watched
                              that famous sasquatch film

hundreds of times, sequestered in your bedroom,
          laying potato chips one
                              at a time on your tongue,
sipping your pilfered beer like a Eucharist.

                    Here Jacob trades
                              his brother's birthright for a cup
of soup. Here the magician seems to catch a bullet
            in his mouth. Here is the single
                              shoe your brother

left behind, a hole worn through the heel. Here
            is the moment when the creature
                              turns and glances
over its terrible shoulder, then disappears forever.

HISTORY OF FIRE

All things, oh priests, are on fire.
The earthquake on your birthday—

car alarms calling each other
like love-sick dogs, the forgotten

air-raid siren on the YMCA yowling
its one, sore note. The decks

of the freeway snap together,
the burning cars trapped. You watch

the rescue workers disappear
into the smoking gaps. Sometimes

they return with a survivor;
sometimes they do not. Begin

with the molecule, its carbons
shoulder to shoulder in the cold

quantum space. Begin 400 million
years ago, the Devonian air blushed

with oxygen, the first lightning-sparked
peat bogs smoldering on the shore.

Begin with this: fuel, oxygen, and heat,
this triangle, this tent of sticks you build

in the dirt. Begin with the room
where they waited until fire wormed

down through the rafters, draped
like a robe across them, until foreign

words clogged their mouths. Parthians
and Elamites, Arabs and Greeks,

all understood, but someone
in the crowd jeered: they are full of wine.

The tongue is burning, oh priests,
its words unhinge their atoms.

From the hotel roof, in Istanbul,
you see it: a tire dump burning

on the other side of the Bosporus,
its base brighter than any city lights.

A waiter brings plates of olives
for your family. You hold your plate,

a cool *O* against your palm.
The moon is rust. The moon is gone.

Kallinikos the alchemist invented
liquid fire, a fluid that ignited

whenever it touched water,
and the Byzantines used it

to burn down the Muslim fleet
surrounding Constantinople.

The recipe for this fire is lost—
petroleum or calcium phosphide cooked

from lime, charcoal, and bones?
You have walked the covered

bazaar, its air rough with tea;
at the newly arrived American

burger chain, you ate your fill.
You stood inside the Blue Mosque,

your mother and aunt covering
their nude arms with burlap shawls

taken from a heap by the door,
while high on a pole, a loudspeaker

warbled out the call to prayer. The eye,
oh priests, is on fire. Everything

it sees is only flame or fuel.
All day, the Santa Ana winds

goad the fire. Neighbors stand
in the cul-de-sac and stare

at the orange ribbon draped
across the hills. You watch

whole groves of eucalyptus
sprout red wings, the trunks

screaming as they split in half.
The fire department hands out

sooty pamphlets that warn *fires
persist in root systems for days*,

and for a week you watch
the backyard maple, waiting

for it to give birth to a hot, angry child.
Fire burns a forest, a home,

a river. Cresting over the hills
at night you see the refinery,

caked in fluorescent light,
its stacks fingering the sky

with purple flames. You know
how close you've come to disaster:

the trio of gulls that disappeared
into the jet engine, a plume

of smoke and blood pouring out
the other side, the guttural heave

of the cabin as the plane
banked hard. Safe on the tarmac,

you looked back and saw
the fuselage feathered with carbon.

Colorado, Arizona, Oregon—
the summer every forest burned,

your brother took a job watching
trees from a stand, a lifeguard

without water. The fires at night,
he said, started like planets,

orange sparks low on the horizon.
After your parents' divorce,

in your father's cramped efficiency,
you opened the oven and flames

filled the small kitchen, crisped
the flesh on your arm and cheek.

All the way to the hospital,
your father chanted an apology.

Agni's parents were two sticks—
rubbed together, they gave birth

to him and then burned to death.
You grow to understand this.

Agni grows up; he has two faces
and seven tongues. You understand

this too. Though it terrifies you,
you even understand when India

builds the Agni missile, capable
of striking targets deep in China.

You grow to understand *credible*
deterrence, every other euphemism

of violence and mistrust, all
the Patriots and Peacekeepers

in the world. Nothing lasts,
oh priests; it turns to smoke

as we speak. Some fires are only
slower than others: a trash fire

catches a vein of coal that spreads
its own dark roots under the town.

The gases buckle the streets,
fill up basements, kill small dogs.

Some people learn to live with it;
most do not. The fire burns

for forty years, until the town
is all but deserted, until only a few

caved-in buildings still lean against
their naked I-beams, until the highway,

like a river, changes its course
to avoid the town. Backpacking

with your father in Arizona
you stop for lunch halfway up

the mountain, where a sign
memorializes a Boy Scout troop

that froze to death on this spot.
You can't imagine dying that way,

not here, where the dusty lizards
pant on the rocks. You had imagined

a desert of scrub brush and cacti,
but when you reach the peak

you see whole forests burning.
Your father tells you that fire

isn't a thing—like a book or a building
or a child—but rather a process

of things, the road a thing walks
to become another, new thing.

Begin with accident or intent, a spark
or a hand. Begin with priests

smoldering in their temples.
Begin with the gods punishing

or rewarding us. Begin with this:
You wake up on a train

inside a tunnel of smoke.
You remember those plane flights

through clouds, miles above
earth, without bearing or reference,

the recirculated air thin as a dream
about leaving. You've passed

the lumber yards, their damp stacks
of logs raw under the sun, the grunting

machine that rearranges them
with its hydraulic claw. You know

that fuel is fuel. Changing the trees
to houses won't save them.

You stand and walk the length
of the train like a drunk, your legs

unsure. It's barely dawn
and the other passengers mumble

half-words in languages you almost
understand. For hours, the train

glides through the smoke, and this
makes it easy to forget where you are,

where you've been, and where you're going.

WHAT LAND
OF
MILK AND HONEY

PORTMANTERRORISM

Would it make a difference to say we suffered
from affluenza in those days? Could we blame
Reaganomics, advertainment, the turducken
and televangelism we swallowed by the sporkful,
all that brunch and Jazzercise, Frappuccinos
we guzzled on the Seatac tarmac, sexcellent
celebutantes we ogled with camcorders while
our imagineers simulcast the administrivia
of our alarmaggedon across the glocal village?
Would it help to say that we misunderestimated
the effects of Frankenfood and mutagenic smog,
to speculate that amid all our infornography
and anticipointment, some crisitunity slumbered
unnoticed in a roadside motel? Does it count
for nothing that we are now willing to admit
that the animatronic monster slouching across
the soundstage of our tragicomic docusoap
was only a distraction? Because now, for all our
gerrymandering, the anecdata won't line up for us.
When we saw those contrails cleaving the sky
above us, we couldn't make out their beginning
or their end. What, in those long hours of ash,
could our appletinis tell us of good or of evil?

MISANTHROPY

The more I love humanity in general, the less I love man in particular.
—Dostoyevsky, *The Brothers Karamazov*

Don't get me wrong. I don't cry over every soggy
        heap of wheat rotting in the field, each
                        sun-bleached
book jacket left for years in the shop window.

        On the news, a child is found
                    bound in a closet,
covered in filth, or clinging to the buoy a mile
        from shore, or expired in the furnace
                    of a sealed car.

Even the mud wasps love the milky grubs tucked
        into the tunnels of the nest. The longer
                        I love
your face, the more hateful each new face becomes.

        We do what we're told. Rest, clean
                    food. Still,
it dies the size of a buckeye, curled salamander
        smoldering in the salty
                  well of our hope.

In the lost pieta, Mary cradles a giant locust,
        a spike driven through its thorax.
                    The river runs
from the mountain where Abraham took his son.

        You and I will descend together
                    into the valley.
The river burns. The people devour one another.
        Even the wolf swallowing the sun
                  is ashamed.

BRIDE BELIEVES TERRORISTS
KIDNAPPED MISSING GROOM

—headline

My sympathy for the bride sours when I read
that they live in Kansas, that her fiancé, a bouncer

at a local bar, is a known gambler and, according
to a longtime friend, not cut out for the married life.

I imagine him on the lam, stopping at every roadside
attraction that doesn't remind him of what he's left

behind. He spends a whole day at Noah's Funland,
where the proprietor asks for only a few dollars.

He walks the gravel footpath to the fiberglass ark,
which is bigger than he expected: plaster giraffes

lean dangerously out of the high windows, and a bear
looks over its shoulder as Noah's sons herd it up

the ramp. Noah stands alone, a lamb in his hard arms.
Teenagers have broken off the lamb's head, and the new

head doesn't match the body—a brown seam of epoxy
circles its throat. On cue, recorded thunder buzzes

from a speaker, rain drizzles from a perforated pipe,
and the groom stands still as the mannequins around him,

waiting for the world to fill up with water. In his hotel
that night he wonders what his fiancée is doing, how she

has explained his absence to their friends. He imagines
her sitting alone in their apartment, holding a cold cup

of coffee, watching a TV show about celebrity weddings.
Every day the mailbox fills with RSVP cards from family

who haven't heard of the missing groom, haven't read
the bride's grim theory in the paper. She's too ashamed

to explain it now, but her theory was only a joke gone
wrong: she told the newspapers that an abduction

was the only excuse she'd accept. She doesn't know
why she said *terrorists*—that was the image that crept

into her head: two men, faces hidden behind kaffiyeh,
jab Kalashnikovs into the groom's ribs as they march

him through a cornfield to a makeshift jail cell inside
a silo. It doesn't matter why they've come to Kansas

or why they've chosen him as their hostage, but every
day that he doesn't come home, they torture him

more brutally: they beat him with iron bars; they insert
electrodes into his eyes; with a pair of pliers, they pluck

his teeth like berries. Afterward, they leave him naked,
shackled to the silo floor, and through a hole in the roof,

he sees the moon for a few minutes each night. Strokes
of distant thunder tremble in the aluminum siding,

and he begins a prayer that is not a prayer but a story
whose ending he can't yet see. In the story, a storm

finds the one small hole above him and slowly floods
the silo. In one telling, he drowns. In another, the silo

bursts, and he is left bobbing on the surface of a new
ocean. But the rain falls so unevenly on the earth,

and he knows that it will not find him, that it will fall
on the lives of men and women he cannot even imagine.

KUZKA'S MOTHER

Now we are all sons of bitches.
        —Kenneth Bainbridge

Inside each matryoshka, you will find another, smaller,
        its cheeks' rosy discs dwindling
                                to pinpricks.
The smallest doll is thumb-thick and sturdy as bone.

        Shiva dipped his big toe
                        into the ocean and started
to churn the water. From this churning, he created
        the weapon of the gods,
                        a spinning disc of fire.

The seasons punish each other in turn for their excesses.
        Even as the glacier grinds the earth
                                down to a prairie
of sameness, grass stubbles up at the lip of retreating ice.

        Inside each person, you
                        will find another, smaller.
On the island where the world's largest bomb
        was tested, the polar sun rises
                        in the shape of a cube.

When the Trinity set down its foot on the desert
        outside Alamogordo, the sand
                        turned into a crater
of glass ten feet deep and a thousand feet across.

        Khrushchev promised to show us
                        Kuzka's mother.
Though the idiom was lost on us, we had our own
        vision of what would emerge when the earth
                                split open.

A COIGN OF VANTAGE

This is the way not to see. The picture you took:
       the blanket
             revoked, L's naked body dappled
in lesions, legs tapered down like a carving

       whittled too far, his mouth
                     the slack *O* in *morphine.*
Above him, a print of Alma-Tadema's
       A Coign of Vantage, the silky Roman ladies

       watching the distant
                  bay for arrivals
and departures, the bronze lion always averting
       its eyes. (Was it later
               that day, the undeveloped

photo still spooled in the camera's dark chamber,
       that you were crossing
                 the bridge and knew—
you said *knew*—that your friend had died?)

       None of the Roman ladies
                speak. The lion
refuses even to breathe. But their vigil is all
       idleness. No worry
              has fixed them to that ledge,

to sit under that sun until their shoulders
       have burned down
             to rusty bone. Weeks later, I saw
the photo, tacked to the wall with your others:

       a snakeskin stirring
               on the gravel road, fists
knuckling a lymphoma of dough, a new
       magnolia blossom already
                 browned at the edges.

L's body among them, though I said nothing.
             You said nothing. I cannot
                              even say if the girl
running the Fotomat machine said anything

             when she slipped that
                              picture into an envelope
and scrawled your name on it with black
             marker. She may have seen
                              much worse.

When we crossed the bay again, if the boats
             below the bridge seemed
                              to write something
on the slate of water, I couldn't read it.

(What I wanted to ask
             was this: did you pull the blanket back
             in order to take
                              the picture?)

THE CRYPTOZOOLOGIST CHAPERONES HIS DAUGHTER'S PROM

From his post by the punch bowl, he tries to track
her movements through the darkened gymnasium,

but he has already forgotten the color of her dress,
its cut indistinguishable from what a dozen other

girls are wearing. He watches the dancers' faces
flutter in and out, each caught by dimes of light

from a battered mirror ball. Those faces could belong
to any of the cryptids he has chased: Jersey Devil,

Pope Lick Monster, Sarasota Skunk Ape. No one
looks quite human in the murky room—mouths

too big or small, limbs stretched out of proportion,
their dance steps a nervous stagger of some other

creature's gait. The illicit cigarettes glowing
by the fire door could be the eyes of the Mothman,

the Bray Road Beast, the Dover Demon.
He guards the drinks from prankish tampering:

hidden flasks of cheap, fumy vodka or, worse, drips
of liquid acid, LSD, PCP. The vice principal

has warned him that anything is possible:
You never know with these kids. He startles

when his daughter and her date lurch out
of the shadows, the elliptical orbit of a slow dance

bringing them finally to his corner of the room.
When the song ends and they break for punch,

he averts his eyes—she has instructed him
to pretend that they are strangers, that he does not

know her. But this is easier than she thinks.
She is a chimera, a lycanthrope, never wholly

one creature, and never the same creature
for long. She calls this *fitting in*, something

he has never understood the need for anyway.
You don't understand what it's like, she says,

you don't know. It's true, he admits, he doesn't.
What he does know: the Chupacabra prefers

the blood of nanny goats, the Loveland Frog
exudes the odor of alfalfa, and the Deer Lake

Sasquatch has only four toes. For these claims
he has some evidence: blurry photos, dubious

eyewitness accounts, plaster casts of tracks
in the mud. For his daughter, he has even less.

He can't trust his own memories of her face
or voice. Books she loved as a child were books

some other child loved. The next song cues up
and she and her date disappear into the fold

of bodies. He watches her as she drifts out
across the wooden floor, sure that when she

returns he will not recognize any part of her.

JUDITH & HOLOFERNES

The brain goes on living, or so they say, for a few
        seconds after the head is
                severed. The tent stays
shut. The sword rusts down to a feather of iron.

      The world isn't
               like the shoebox dioramas built
by schoolchildren: the balcony scene, three ships
        approaching the shore, soldiers
                  raising a flag.

No one painted Bethulia's grain sheaved in rows,
        the neat teepees of spears
                stacked by the barracks.
Who can name the men who share Lorca's grave?

      On the bus I notice a man wearing
                a shirt that says
"I ♥ My M-16." Who can say if Judith began to love
        Holofernes the moment sword gritted
                against bone?

Walking at night, I always glance at my neighbors'
        windows and half expect to see
                a fierce struggle,
like Jacob wrestling in the nameless arms of an angel.

      One day Nikolai Yezhov
                walked beside Stalin
along the Volga, and the next day he never existed.
        Judith's husband died
                bringing in the harvest.

THE PINCH

Pinching pennies, your mother called it, but how
could that describe the way your father shadowed

each of you through the house, flipping off lights
the moment you left a room? He turned off the TV

whenever you left the couch for a soda—not
from the fridge, reserved only for things that spoiled,

but out of the box in the pantry. True, he was faithful
to his own dogma—he drank his beer warm

but always talked it away, saying that was how
it was meant to be savored, that coldness only

covered shitty flavor. A good beer you could drink
hot as your own blood, and it wouldn't matter,

though of course his beer was no good. It came
in gold cans, no label, no name, no company willing

to claim it. Half the time the pull tabs broke off
and he punched the tops open with a screwdriver,

then suckled at the foaming hole. Who could bear
the way his finger probed the coin return slot

of every payphone or vending machine he passed?
Who could forgive cut-rate sneakers with soles

that pealed off on the summer blacktop, cheap
fillings that howled when you opened your mouth

in winter? Who could swallow off-brand Spam,
or endure the swiftness with which he bent over

for anything resembling a penny, pressing that
grimy surface to his lips before stowing it

in his shirt pocket? Those were our lean days,
your mother reminds you now. But what other

father pushed his car home the last quarter mile
every night because you lived at the bottom

of the hill and why waste that precious vapor
of gas when gravity would do the work for you?

Can you still see him cresting the hill, right hand
on the wheel, left hand braced on the open door,

both feet raging against the pavement? How
was it that you described the moment he jumped

in and slammed the door, that long minute
you waited while he coasted down to you?

THE MARIAN APPARITIONS

On the moldy shower curtain, the Virgin rendered
      in pointillist dots of mildew—you must

                                        step back
to see it, and her expression shifts as a breeze

      from the open window twists
                      the plastic sheet: frown to smile to
frown. For every miracle at Lourdes, thousands
      go home as crippled or sick
                   as before—lungs

still clogged with gooey cysts, blood like wet coffee grounds,
      air in the bones. The odds are
              better at home,
in the hospital, but believers have never had much
        faith
      in the odds. To look at one thing and see

another. The Mother in a tree stump, a sandwich,
      a government building in Clearwater.
                  The miracle is not
the mistake but the mistake's persistence. The face

      I think I see in the crowd
            at the bus depot dissolves
into a stranger's face. Thousands clot the lawn
      to see the Virgin fading through
              the side of the church,

until the minister, tired of the foot traffic, scrapes
      away the paint to reveal an old
             advertisement, Boxcar Willie.
Our eyes pick faces from the mush of photons, a hand

      grasping the right end of a knife without
               thinking.
But this is only metaphor: one thing is not really
      the other no matter how badly I wish
            it were so. We are
hardwired to recognize faces—the unresponsive infant
      is abandoned, or so the logic goes.

But what, in the end, is necessary
to a face? If scar or defect wipes away an eye, a lip,
a nose: when does what we see

cease to be what we know?
To look at one thing. The finer particles tell us that looking

changes what we see. But we knew
this already, how the particular
saints attend our particular needs. If not the Mother,
then her well-worn son:
a lime stain on a Chicago
underpass, blessing the masses that surge past him

on their way to work, or glowering
from the Eagle Nebula,
a place already named for something it is not. Metaphor
works that way, linking what we know

to what we don't,
though the lie of poetry saves no more lives than the lie
of prayer. A birthmark. A bruise.
The gory Rorschach
of a red river delta seen from a plane. For every
piece of falling fruit we catch,
a hundred others

find the ground and rot. And what we do catch fares no better.
What does it mean, even if
the Virgin really is in that peach pit,
that dirty bed sheet? Does she bless or curse
the things she touches?

When the radiologist pinned
the X-ray to the light, I saw two lakes at night, the water
choppy. *Do you see them?* he asked
as one by one
he circled the small dark boats with his finger.

THE CRICKET IN THE BASEMENT

It chirps all night somewhere behind the empty boxes,
        but when I close in, spare boot
                        in hand, it goes quiet.
Before he was a prophet, Joseph Smith dowsed for gold.

        Outside, the moon is always
                        falling. The tethered dog
rubs his circle of lawn raw. God showed Moses
        the land that he would never
                        be allowed to enter.

While searching for Quivira, Coronado was thrown
        from his horse and went insane.
                        The cicadas sing
about the years they've spent sleeping in the earth.
        The man in the blizzard passes
                        within arm's reach
of his cabin and does not see it. Joseph Smith
        was shot to death as he tried
                        to jump from a window.

Zeno's arrow hangs motionless in the air; Achilles
        cannot catch the tortoise. Every aim
                        is an asymptote,
and the blind spot is in the center of the human eye.

THE SOUL DIVA, PAST HER PRIME, VISITS THE HOLY LAND

We watched her somber, shawl-wrapped penitence
beside the Wailing Wall, her procession

through Jerusalem's yellowed streets,
her entourage in the grim attitude of pilgrims.

Later, from the stairs of her private jet,
she swept a gloved hand out over the tarmac,

the attendant paparazzi. She said:
This is my land! Back home, in a lawn chair

she stared into a camera and told us
how the trip had changed her life. *My roots,*

she said, *run deep in that place.* We heard
the interviewer, out of frame, asking

about D——, her husband, the black eye
that hummed purple when he slapped

her behind such and such a bar: White
Lotus, the Viper Room, Garden of Eden—

accounts differ. *I love my husband,*
she chanted. *I love him.* The interviewer

pressed on, asking almost everything
we had ever wanted to know. Did she

have a coke habit? Was she anorexic?
All she said: *I will never be fat.* Then no one

spoke as her eyes trolled some horizon
behind and beyond the camera. The whole lawn

seethed in the mush of its soft focus.
In a kitchen, miles away, someone dropped

a slice of lunch meat—it smacked the linoleum
like a kiss. In another city, someone

masturbated in a public bathroom.
People died various, unrecorded deaths.

In a room alone, someone watched
the diva's first film: in the finale,

her wood-lipped leading man stood by
as she howled song after song, each given

to the crowd, but each also secretly
for him, and we waited breathless to see

if he would reach out and catch
the quivering line of her voice.

CHALLENGER

The bones of Hannibal's elephants can still be found
        in the Alps. The tilting, prairie
                    homesteads where our
tragedies are born will become historical monuments.

        Crows carry off
             the breadcrumbs, and the lost children
have only a trail of guttering stars to guide them home.
        In Vinland the Vikings left behind
                    coins, combs, nails.

Max Q is the value at which aerodynamic stress peaks,
        the moment when a rising vessel's
                integrity is tested.
Nothing is a tragedy these days until it is on television.

        The first animals sent into outer space
                    died of fear.
A poisoned arrow killed Ponce de León. One day
        a person will walk out
                of his home and not return.

The Millerites waited for God on their rooftops
        like birds wait for dawn.
                The crowds are already
gathering to see the crooked plume of smoke.

        In the deep sea dark, some fish lost
                the power of sight;
some grew eyes big as hubcaps; others began to glow.
        The wreckage of *Challenger* washed
                ashore for ten years.

LOVE LETTER FROM ZION
NATIONAL PARK, UTAH

We can only enter
        the park through a tunnel. At the entrance, the rangers tell the
biggest RVs to turn back—they are too large to enter the promised land.
We see the burning faces of the spurned travelers as they swirl up dust in
the turnaround, how they will not meet our eyes as they drive away. The
eye of the needle—we remember, oh lord, how few pass through it. And
we are our own camels, our high-tech backpacks sloshing their bladders of
bitter water as we ascend the paved switchbacks toward
        who knows what. We have seen your wonders of stone, oh lord:
the Sentinel, the Court of the Patriarchs, the Great White Throne, the
slim Virgin River that carved them. From the top of Angel's Landing, the
park unfolds like some messiah's dirt-red robe. Below, the fearless deer
stroll through our campsites, dipping their delicate necks into the trash
cans and unattended coolers. We can just make out the lonely blue nipple
of our tent, the drip of cars winding into the park. We cannot see
        the places we've been: Provo, West Jordan, Devil's Slide, Moab,
Providence, Goshen, Moroni, Jerusalem, Enoch, or even Salt Lake City,
where, in the mall, an eight-foot fiberglass Christ belted out beatitudes
from a tinny speaker hidden somewhere in his body. He said so much we
knew already. But he said nothing about those turned back at the gates of
paradise. What compass point do they follow as their looming caravans
roar through the desert? What land of milk and honey

                                                awaits them,
                                                oh lord?

BACK TO EARTH
UNHARMED

COLLECTIVE

I have said nothing of an unkindness of ravens,
      your finger on the map, smudging
                      the Zagros,
worrying the crease that splits North America.

      The chorus of martyrs
                  is waiting in the wings
for the note that will cue their entrance, their
      grand finale. Even the locusts
                    are embarrassed.

Any piano bar player will tell you not to start
      the first song with an empty
                  tip jar. Any thug
knows it's safest to throw the second stone.

      It's no accident they call
                  a group of baboons
a congress. A heresy of vultures. An obfuscation
      of doves. Thrift of eagles. Temple
                  of worms.

It doesn't take the Delphic oracle to decipher
      scrapes on the guard rail
                  or a burned-out
Humvee smoking along the road to the city.

      A misfortune of boots,
                  a catastrophe of hands.
But don't forget that when the map is folded,
      our country touches theirs, face
                  against face.

BATTLE OF ALEXANDER AT ISSUS

Off in the mountains a hermit checks
his rabbit traps before returning
to his hut for the night. The rabbits grow
bold near dawn and dusk, the hours
when clouds lower ladders of light
down the mountainsides. The hermit
hasn't admired this light in decades.
At this time of day he is always bent
low, unfastening the thin leather snares
from around still-warm necks. If he hears
what sounds like thunder in the valley
one cloudless evening as he ties another
limp body to his belt, he thinks only
of returning home to bed, the rabbit fleas
that torment his sleep, the door that never
quite closes against the cold night air.

CONDITIONAL

We all have them, the lucky cousins. Feckless, blessed.
    One backed over by a bulldozer, treads
                          up to his chin.
Not a bone broken, not a bruise. Sunk in the soft mud.

    What can be said about grace
                that does not diminish it?
To play a drunk, the best actors pretend to be sober.
    The street mime ladles water
              from his leaky canoe.

Of the blind dog and the three-legged rabbit he chases, only
    one can be lucky tonight. Our cousins race
                  every train
to its crossing on principle; it's no surprise they win.

    If you had been born to different parents,
            would your stomach still
be cratered with cigarette burns? Let us believe rain
    follows the plow, that the luck
           we earn is indivisible.

Let me believe that the porch security light recognizes
    my particular shape approaching
               the house at night.
Termites carry our poison back to their many cousins.

    Canoeing under the broken
            train bridge, we looked up
and saw a golden bird spray-painted on the belly
    of the trestle, gaps of sunlight
          punctuating the wings.

THE YEAR WE BLEW UP THE WHALE—
FLORENCE, OREGON

In that same year, after Lefty Watson missed
his third straight placekick against Salem High,

we rushed the field. Lefty's father, in a black
and orange track suit, shimmied up the goal posts

and, beating the air with his fists, incited
what the *Umpqua Register* would later call

a riot. But the Salem team walked off the field
unharmed, if a bit confused, as we stayed behind

to rip out every inch of turf. In that same year,
when the single-vessel fleet of the Devil Ray

Fishing Company returned with an empty hold,
the owner took a five-pound sledge to the keel

and let the ship sink. In that same year, when
Pamela Reese learned she would never have

children, she stopped throwing anything away,
and slowly her house filled up with garbage,

distended bags of it clotting the hallways, bags
sagging the attic beams, bags overflowing

through the windows onto the reeking lawn.
In that same year, when Ambrose Hecklin's only

son was run over by a pickup truck, Ambrose drove
all the way to Lincoln City, walked up to the first

car salesman he could find, and shot him
in the face. In that same year, when Nell Barrett,

last speaker of the Siuslaw language, died alone
in her two-room bungalow, her estranged son

showed up at the county clinic the next morning
with a mouth full of blood, and though outsiders

would later claim he'd accidentally bitten off
his own tongue in a drunken fit, we knew

the truth before the doctor found the filet knife
in his coat pocket. So when the dead whale

washed up on our beach, of course we tried
to blow it up. The newscasters, who'd come

from as far as Portland when they heard our plan,
were shocked when the blast only carved out

a U-shaped hole in the animal's stomach.
The out-of-towners, who had come to gawk

and jeer, ran for cover as basketball-sized chunks
of whale rained on the parking lot a hundred yards

away. But we were not in the least bit shaken.
If we have learned anything from this, said

our city engineers, standing on the beach in their
gory parkas, it is that we need more dynamite.

TEACH A MAN TO FISH

They say that in forty years the oceans will be empty,
                    every fish eaten, but yesterday
                                        in Kansas a farmer
fell into a silo and died smothered by his own grain.

            Teach a man to fish, and he will
                                        burn down his house.
Shelter the elk so your sons may shoot him; save trees
            to burn another day; eat to be
                                        hungry tomorrow.

When the river flooded, we canoed through the fields
            to catch the carp that thrashed
                                        among the cornstalks.
In the years of drought, we portaged over the shoals.

            The roots and bugs have uses
                                        for the dog and cow.
The fields of Kansas were once covered in water,
            and may be again, though we won't
                                        live to see it.

My grandfather is always angling for more time alone
            on his boat, out of earshot.
                                        The oil derrick keeps
its creaking beat by the road though the well is long dry.

            The catfish spreads its barbs
                                        to choke the heron
that has swallowed it. Lying in its cave, the body
            of Jesus longed only for the mist
                                        on the sea of Galilee.

TRYING TO CROSS THE BORDER,
THE WAR CORRESPONDENT IS JAILED

They don't strip him nude, march him blindfolded
to the yard, hold the pistol to his head,

let the hammer tap an empty chamber—
not even that. Their violence is without

malice, a few perfunctory fists jabbed
like junk letters through the mail slot back home.

Will he even bruise? They don't video
him mumbling their demands through swollen lips.

They won't even tell him the conditions
of his release, what or how much his friends

or government must pay for him, his worth
rounded down to a dollar sum, number

of their own they want freed. The one jailer
who speaks any English can only say

a few words of it—*you, me, eat, sleep, now*—
and speaks them as if he can't bear to say

anything more. There are no 3 a.m.
interrogations, demands for secrets

he doesn't know. They keep him for six days
and then let him go: two men he doesn't

recognize drive him out to the road
where he was first arrested. When he gets out

of the jeep, one man hands him his wallet
and points toward the horizon. They make

a lightning U-turn and tear off into
the desert. He walks down the road, flipping

through his wallet, which is empty. No cash,
no credit cards, not even his many

identifications, visas he needs to cross
this border or that, each one stamped

with the evidence of his last passage,
neon insignias of what he's done.

THE GIANT SQUID

One morning, the refugee sees his old tormentor buying bread
    at the corner market. The loaves swaddled
                like infants
born in secret prisons and given to the colonels' barren wives.

    The giant squid, when pulled onto the deck,
              died immediately.
It has three hearts and the largest eyes in the world. Our hearts
    are as unsteady as the hands
        of the old dictator as he awaited trial.

At night, planes dropped the bodies of the disappeared over
    the ocean. For years, scientists could only
        extrapolate the giant squid
from beaks they cut from the bellies of beached whales.

    The guards at the prison camp kept
        rabbits on which they doted.
The assassin is a skinny teenager with a five-dollar haircut;
    the marshals carry him weeping
        to and from the courthouse.

Among the generalissimo's crimes was this: he made a man
    swallow teeth the guards had taken
        from his wife and son.
Waking in bed at night, our own bodies often startle us.

    Shipwreck survivors said the giant squid
        could lift a boat
from the water and break it like a loaf of bread. Even Nemo,
    whose name means *no one*, felt
        a fathoms-deep regret.

ARC WELDING LESSON

Do you see my arms,
   the little craters
where sparks bit down,

like the moon, like tracks
of a rabbit in the snow?

The sound, there isn't a word
for it. If you could clamp
   jumper cables

   to a cicada's legs,
that is the sound the arc
would make.

If you could listen
   to what the radio listens to
when the radio is turned off,

it would be that sound.

   It's like saying "yes"
and being dipped

in tar: nodding, putting down
that mask.

The electrode pulls toward
   the surface—it is your job
to pull away gently, only

a little, only enough.
   Treat it like a letter

you're writing home
   from a war: lying
in your dim berth,

your nub of a pencil hovering
            above the page.

How can you say that if,
            given a chance,
you would not touch

            her, quite? You would hold
your fingertips motionless

above her skin and wait
            for some spark to cross

the gap between you?

The electrode is consumed,
            the flux is consumed,
            the surface
is consumed. The arc

mingles them, weds them together
            even as they burn away.

            Strike the arc as if
you were striking your last match

in a blizzard. Strike the arc
            as if you're touching
a woman for the first time.

Or the last.

Once I looked into the arc
            —only a moment—
and for two nights a smoldering

            grain of sand sat behind
each of my eyes. I drank myself

to sleep, and my wife tied
my hands to my sides to keep me

from rubbing my eyelids off.

It is the same thing
        as snow blindness.
It is the reason God hid Moses

in a gap of rock,
only to look out and see
        what?

Lift the mask.
        See the weld running

        like a scar, raised, pale,
crooked, skipping here

and there, thick
        and slow in the middle.
Here is the file to scrape

away the slag. You must
        be careful also,

when you go outside,
not to look too soon

at the white gravel road
        threading down the hill.
You must not look

at the house, that eye-ache
        of whiteness, that day-ghost.

Look first at a tree,
        the dark, writhing

heart of it, and wait.

SETI

The snow sliding loose of the eave is a shibboleth.
    In Arecibo, where they are still
                listening for aliens,
it is 70 degrees tonight, and the moon is booming.

    The cowboys used to bend
                their heads to the earth
and listen for the sound of horses. Only the Indians
    could tell whether the horses
                were coming or going.

The radio telescope is an alms bowl. The stars
    jabber like backyard gossips.
                The thread of gravity
is just strong enough to tether the comets to us.

    A chemical trail leads the ant
                back to his mound;
the bat follows his own voice in the dark. If God has
    a voice, it is sibilant as the static
                between stations.

My mind's room is too small. Why do we care
    which direction our buried dead
                face? Love
is carried piecemeal, as the ant carries everything.

    In the bed at night your sleeping curve
                is a comma
or a comet, the tail of your legs bending toward
    the center of the universe, a bright,
                slow pause.

THE AGING SCI-FI ACTOR SPEAKS TO THIRD GRADERS AT THE LOCAL PLANETARIUM

He waves an arm at the projected stars,
telling them how his childhood love

of space landed him first behind a telescope
and then on a soundstage, which isn't

quite true, but the kids aren't listening
anyway. Maybe their older brothers, stoned

in the basement, watch his show's late-night
reruns, laughing at the recycled plots,

the endless shtick. But these kids don't care.
Drowsing on the carpeted benches, each one

tugs a parent's sleeve. They find him
about as convincing as a plastic spaceship

on a string, floating across a firmament
of black velvet. To them, outer space bristles

with glossy satellites, real as a car
or dog. They yawn the yawns of experts

who know that the cure for delusion is rarely
truth, but rather, a better lie. The planetarium's

dusk hides it all, but he knows the stale smell
of disbelief and boredom. He's seen

the costumed extras, smoking on the backlot,
cigarettes pinched between huge foam fingers,

nothing to read in the rigor of their rubber faces:
blue or green, scaled or hairy. He's seen

the other actors and their stand-ins, doppelgängers
all half an inch shorter and five pounds heavier,

each one wearing someone else's haircut
badly. He wants to tell these children that over

the years he's learned the high-seas pitch
of the spaceship set, its hydraulic legs tossing

the cast from their seats and head-first
into Plexiglas console screens, tell them how

he speaks half his lines at a pale blue rectangle,
trusting that some face will appear there later,

that some editor will dub in another voice,
friend or alien, to answer his own.

THE LAST WORDS OF PANCHO VILLA

Thomas Edison, his body unwinding
on a bed in Menlo Park, turned his head

toward the window. *It's very beautiful
over there*, he said. I imagine him

lying on a litter of the flotsam and jetsam
of invention, his delicate head propped

on an old phonograph cylinder. What
is the recording? An assistant singing?

The long, low whistle of a distant train?
A projector chatters as it throws an image

against the wall: a man sneezing, another
performing the Ghost Dance, a team

of assistants electrocuting an elephant.
What did he see through that window,

and when he called it beautiful, did he
wish he was somewhere or someone else,

that the world in which he was dying
was not beautiful at all? It's easy

to imagine this, though I don't know
much about Edison, or anyone, really,

though I like to believe that listening
brings us closer, sometimes against

our will. I can't help but love the jokes
of killers with a sense of humor,

condemned men of vaudevillian wit.
As they strapped him into the chair,

Appel said: *Well, gentlemen, you*
are about to see a baked apple.

And French, when his turn came,
said: *How about this for a headline?*

French fries. Even the worst villains
sometimes have a gift for poetry.

Standing at the gallows, Carl Panzram
said: *I wish the whole human race*

had one neck and I had my hands on it.
I can't argue with such deft aphorisms,

no matter how venomous. Words
work that way, ratcheting us closer

to one another, even as the gaps
between us grow wider and more

perilous. Amelia Earhart beamed
her voice out into the ear-less lull

of radio waves: *We must be on you,*
but we cannot see you. Fuel

is running low. I wonder if she knew
that no one would answer back,

that while her words found someone,
she would not be found? And if

she had known, what would she toss
into the pool of air and static?

A letter to a secret lover, a testament
of faith, or something more mundane?

Would she beg for the last pages
of a book left unfinished on land,

an apple from a certain orchard,
or to hold a glass of cold tea against

her wrist? I would believe any
of this—we want the smallest pleasures

most of all, don't we? Conrad Hilton,
dying, said only: *Leave the curtain*

on the inside of the tub. Thomas Grasso,
murderer, complained: *I did not get*

my SpaghettiOs. I got spaghetti.
I want the press to know this. Details

matter, even when we're dying;
we ask the condemned for last words

because to deny them that, somehow,
seems worse than death. Einstein's

last words vanished into his nurse's
ignorant ear like a stone thrown down

a long, dry well—she mistook his German
for babble. And even with four gospels,

the Christians can't get their Messiah's
last breath straight, though I suppose

it makes sense to keep their options
open, to reserve those different verses—

despair or resignation—for the days
that need them. Most tragic of all,

however, are those who have nothing
to say, no word to draw us close

one last time. Seven riflemen shot
Pancho Villa while he was driving

through Parral, his roadster loaded
down with gold, flanked by bodyguards.

I imagine this scene as the finale
of an epic western film, Villa staggering

into the dusty street to fire a shot
at one of the riflemen, who crumples

and falls from the roof to the wooden
sidewalk. One of Villa's Dorades,

his golden ones, closer to Villa than
any other—a cousin perhaps—rushes

over and, weeping, lifts the revolutionary
by his bandoliers, whispers something

into his ear. Villa, coughing blood,
delivers a monologue—inspirational,

but short—and dies. Of course,
this does not happen. Death is never

as romantic as we hope. In reality,
Villa has no time for soliloquies,

only time to say: *Don't let it end
like this. Tell them I said something.*

A WINTER OF SITTING BY THE WINDOW

Who can begrudge the labor of the root as it noses
            its way down to the septic tank?
                                    One life can spoil
another. Even some leeches care for their young.

            The storm's curlicue. As seen
                        from space, like milk
swirling in tea. I spend all night counting the birches
            chalked like tally marks
                                along the far, dark hill.

Why listen to the complaint the snow plows grind
            up and down the frozen street?
                                    The clouds mumble.
The ice-laden trees bow and scrape like penitents.

            The tight-haunched rabbit
                        knows that even disaster
demands prayer. And who doesn't cheer for crows
            baiting a hawk, for the inversion
                                of familiar tragedy?

As if holding our grief in abeyance, the lake waits
            till spring to release
                        the bodies of the drowned.
The septic tank breaks, the trees bloom early.

            A hawk snatches our cat
                        from the yard and flies
all the way across the road before changing its mind
            and letting the cat fall back to earth
                                    unharmed.